GENDER IDENTITY for KIDS

A Book About Finding Yourself,
Understanding Others,
and Respecting Everybody!

Andy Passchier

LITTLE, BROWN AND COMPANY
New York Boston

About This Book

The illustrations for this book were created digitally. This book was edited by Andrea Colvin and Aria Balraj, and designed by Sasha Illingworth and Patrick Hulse. The production was supervised by Bernadette Flinn, and the production editor was Marisa Finkelstein. The text was set in Excelsior LT Std, and the display type is hand lettered.

Little, Brown and Company
Hachette Book Group
1290 Avenue of the Americas, New York, NY 10104
Visit us at LBYR.com

First Edition: June 2023

Little, Brown and Company is a division of Hachette Book Group, Inc. The Little, Brown name and logo are trademarks of Hachette Book Group, Inc.

The publisher is not responsible for websites (or their content) that are not owned by the publisher.

Little, Brown and Company books may be purchased in bulk for business, educational, or promotional use. For information, please contact your local bookseller or the Hachette Book Group Special Markets Department at special.markets@hbgusa.com.

Library of Congress Cataloging-in-Publication Data
Names: Passchier, Andy, author.
Title: Gender identity for kids : a book about finding yourself, understanding others, and respecting everybody! / Andy Passchier.
Description: First edition. | New York : Little, Brown and Company, 2023. | Audience: Ages 7–10 | Summary: "This book introduces different terms for gender identity and expression, while also teaching children how to accept and respect others." —Provided by publisher.
Identifiers: LCCN 2022031748 | ISBN 9780316411226 (hardcover) | ISBN 9780316411325 (ebook)
Subjects: LCSH: Gender identity—Juvenile literature.
| Gender expression—Juvenile literature. | Respect for persons—Juvenile literature.
Classiffication: LCC HQ18.552 .P37 2023 | DDC 305.3—dc23/eng/20220804
LC record available at https://lccn.loc.gov/2022031748

ISBNs: 978-0-316-41122-6 (hardcover), 978-0-316-41132-5 (ebook),
978-0-316-56720-6 (ebook), 978-0-316-56723-7 (ebook)

Printed in China • APS • 10 9 8 7 6 5 4 3 2 1

HI THERE!

I'm so glad you're here.
This book is all for you!

TASHA
SHE/HER

VERONICA
SHE/HER

BILLY
HE/HIM

MAX
THEY/THEM

FINN
HE/SHE/THEY

This book will...

★ Help you understand what gender identity means

★ Introduce you to different gender identities

★ Give examples of ways people express their gender

★ Give examples of some harmful behavior that relates to gender identity

★ Teach you how to be respectful and accepting of others

★ Give you some tools to stand up for yourself and others

★ Help you find support if you need it

As we grow up, we're taught lots of messages about gender and that there are certain things we should do, be, or want based on how other people see us: girl or boy, woman or man.

MAN UP!

SUCH A STRONG BOY.

BOYS WILL BE BOYS.

WHAT A PRETTY GIRL.

HI, BEAUTIFUL PRINCESS.

It starts with people talking to us in a different tone or about different things, deciding what toys we should play with, what we should wear, what we should do as a hobby….You may not notice it, but these messages are things you hear over and over, and you might start to believe they're true.

Most kids have at least some idea of what gender feels like for them by the time they turn three or four years old.

BUT WHAT IS GENDER?

WHAT DOES IT ALL MEAN?

5

This book is going to define that, and a lot of other big words, in a way that will make them easier to understand.

Some of the meanings, like words about identities, might change over time, or people might have different meanings for them depending on their own feelings.

It's okay to take a break at any point. Here are some things you could do:

TALK TO SOMEBODY.

DO A FUN DANCE!

HUG A PET OR A STUFFED ANIMAL

DRAW A PICTURE.

GET SOME FRESH AIR.

This book also has *a lot* of questions you can ask yourself or talk about with people you trust.

It's okay if these questions feel overwhelming. You can skip ones you don't want to answer right now and come back to them later, or just continue reading and don't answer them at all!

This book is for you and you can use it however you like.

Okay, maybe just...don't throw it out the window.

Take care of yourself first. The book's not going anywhere.

WHEEEE!!!

CHAPTER 1
SEX vs. GENDER

When people use the word *gender*, sometimes it's hard to know what they're talking about.

Think of when a baby is about to be born. What's the first thing people usually ask?

Adults will say they're talking about the gender of the baby, but actually, they're talking about the sex.

Your sex is decided by doctors and is based on a combination of inside and outside parts.

Most of the time, when a baby is born, sex is based on the way that baby looks on the outside, and usually it goes like this:

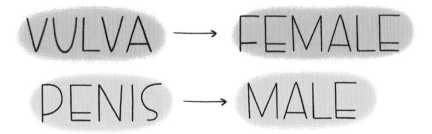

This is called your assigned sex at birth, meaning it was given to you when you were born.

AFAB → assigned female at birth
Doctors looked at you when you were born and decided you were mostly female.

AMAB → assigned male at birth
Doctors looked at you when you were born and decided you were mostly male.

A lot of people think these are the only ways to exist, but this isn't always right.

Some people's bodies at birth can't be described as just female or just male.

Maybe they have different combinations of body parts on the inside and outside. Other times, it's not super clear whether their genitals are a penis or a vulva.

These people would be called intersex.

WHAT'S THAT WORD?

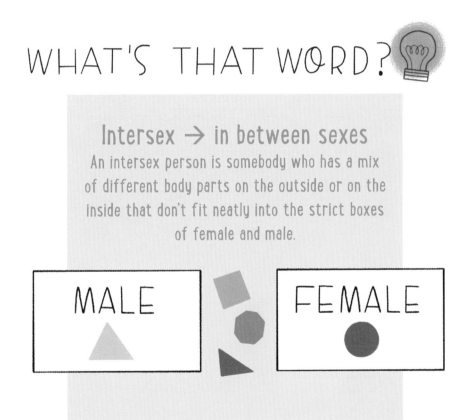

Intersex → in between sexes
An intersex person is somebody who has a mix of different body parts on the outside or on the inside that don't fit neatly into the strict boxes of female and male.

MALE   FEMALE

Sometimes when somebody is born intersex, doctors call them female or male anyway based on how their body parts look on the outside.

Other times, doctors even choose to make changes through surgery so a person fits more easily into a female or male box.

The person themselves doesn't really have a say in this—they're just a baby at this point!

Intersex people and people who stand up for them believe that the person themselves *should* have a say, and are working toward ending surgeries on intersex babies.

Now that we've explained what *sex* means, it's time to move on to our other friend in this chapter: gender!

Gender is **different** from your body.

Gender is . . .

★ How you see yourself

★ How you feel about your body

★ How other people see

★ How you would like other people to see you and talk about you

★ What you like to do and wear

★ How you relate to what people think of when they say "girl" or "boy"

In simple terms:

- ★ Sex comes from your body.

- ★ Gender comes from you!

People often think that your body parts decide your gender and that the two will always match.

But this isn't true for everyone! In the next chapter, we'll talk about lots of different words people can use to describe their genders.

The words *girl* and *boy* come with all sorts of ideas attached to them.

People often think that being a girl or a boy should decide certain traits:

★ What we wear

★ What we do and like

★ How we act

★ How other people talk to us

Here are some examples:

GIRLS LIKE PINK.
BOYS LIKE BLUE.

GIRLS LIKE DOLLS.
BOYS LIKE TRUCKS.

GIRLS WEAR SKIRTS AND DRESSES.
BOYS WEAR PANTS.

GIRLS WEAR JEWELRY
AND MAKEUP.
BOYS DON'T.

GIRLS HAVE LONG HAIR.
BOYS HAVE SHORT HAIR.

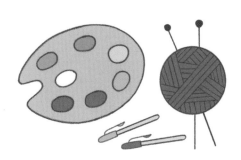
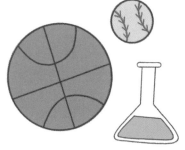

GIRLS ARE BETTER AT ARTS AND CRAFTS.
BOYS ARE BETTER AT SPORTS AND SCIENCE.

These expectations are usually put on us before we are even born, like when a person buys a pink or a blue gift for the future parent of a baby.

These gender expectations, or gender roles as they're sometimes called, don't just apply when we're kids. They happen to adults too! We'll read more about this in chapter 3.

WHAT'S THAT WORD?

Gender roles are the idea that people should behave a certain way or do certain activities based on their gender and assigned sex at birth.

These rules about gender were made up by other people and have been developed over a long time, but they haven't always been true!

For example, in the US in the 1920s, pink used to be the color for boys and blue was the color for girls. This didn't change until the 1940s! And doesn't it seem silly that our interests, behaviors, and what we should want in life are all influenced by what our body parts look like when we're born?

NOW WE KNOW

The important thing to learn from this chapter is that sex and gender are *not* the same thing.

Sex refers to parts of your body, while gender refers to how you feel.

People often think there are only two sexes and two genders, and that they always have to match in each person. As we've already seen, there are lots more ways for people to exist.

Also, just because your body looks a certain way doesn't mean you will want to live up to all the expectations people have made up about living in that body.

QUESTIONS

♡ What did doctors and adults call you when you were born? Do you think they got it right? Did they get anything wrong?

♡ What things have you been taught are just for girls? Or just for boys?

♡ Have you ever been told something you did, wanted, or liked wasn't for your assigned sex? How did that make you feel?

♡ Have you ever noticed adults around you behave in a certain way? Do you think this might be based on gender roles? How so?

CHAPTER 2
GENDER IDENTITY

In this chapter, we're going to explore lots of different words people can use to describe their gender, sometimes also called gender identity.

ALL DIFFERENT & EQUALLY VALID

Having a gender assigned to you at birth, along with your sex, is a little bit like having your favorite color picked for you.

Imagine it had to be either red or blue, and you could never ever change it.

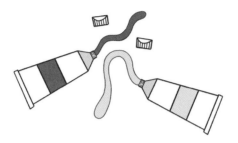

Maybe you were given blue and that actually turned out to be your favorite color.

AMAZING! GOOD FOR YOU!

But, as you might suspect, it doesn't work that way for everybody, and the world is filled with many more amazing colors.

What if you were assigned blue as a favorite color when you were born, but as you grew up, you realized you liked red? Or the other way around?

Maybe you like both, or you like mixing them together and making purple.

You can like blue on some days but red on others.

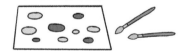

You might like other colors, like yellow, green, orange, or pink!

Maybe you're super adventurous and you'd like to try mixing your own color that doesn't exist yet.

And maybe you love **ALL** the colors of the rainbow.

All these are great options, and the same thing goes for gender.

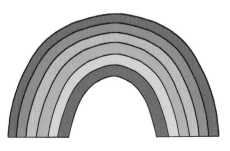

All the color or gender options together make up what we call the gender spectrum.

WHAT'S THAT WORD?

The gender spectrum is the idea that gender exists beyond just "woman" and "man," and that people can exist somewhere along a gradient or outside of it entirely.

Most people are expected to have a gender identity that matches their assigned sex. Your gender identity *can* be the same as your sex, but it can also be completely different!

Let's take a look at some of these words and identities.

READY TO DIVE IN?

GENDER TREASURE!

For some people, the gender that adults picked for them when they were born matches how they feel.

This is TASHA.

When Tasha was born, doctors said she was a girl. This means Tasha's assigned sex at birth is female. As Tasha grew up, she was comfortable with this word.

She lives her life being called a girl, and this feels fine and makes her happy!

This means Tasha is cisgender.

WHAT'S THAT WORD?

To be cisgender means that your gender identity is the same as the sex you were assigned at birth.

OOH! I GET IT!

Cis → on the same side as
Gender → the gender you were assumed to be

For others, the gender that adults picked for them when they were born doesn't feel right.

This is VER◯NICA.

When Veronica was born, doctors said she was a boy.

This means Veronica's assigned sex at birth is male.

As she got older, Veronica noticed she didn't like it when adults referred to her as a boy.

Despite being called a boy, Veronica knew she was a girl.

This means Veronica is transgender!

WHAT'S THAT WORD?

To be transgender means that your gender identity is different from the sex you were assigned at birth.

Trans → across from
Gender → the gender you were assumed to be

Sometimes people are older when they realize they might be trans (the shortened word for *transgender*). They might not know it's even an option, or maybe they don't feel ready to think about it.

And sometimes people realize they might not be a girl *or* a boy at all!

There are many more possible identities besides girl and boy, just like there are many other favorite colors besides red and blue.

The idea that there are only two gender options for people is called the gender binary.

WHAT'S THAT WORD?

A binary is something that has two parts.

Bi- in front of a word means "two"!

The gender binary says that out of all the identities, girl and boy are the only ones that are real and the only ones that count.

Sometimes people say there are only two kinds of bodies, so there should be only two kinds of gender identities, but as we saw in chapter 1, that's not true at all!

A gender identity that falls outside of this binary is called nonbinary.

WHAT'S THAT WORD?

Nonbinary identities fall outside of the binary of girl and boy.

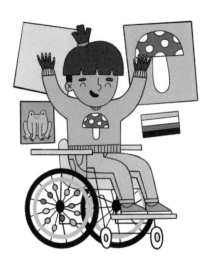

This is MAX.

Max doesn't feel like they really fit into the box of being a girl or a boy.

They prefer gender-neutral language.

WHAT'S THAT WORD?

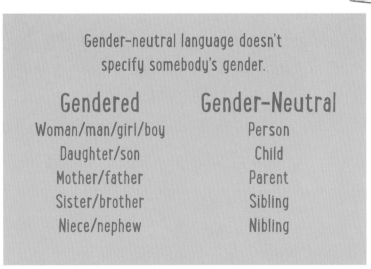

Gender-neutral language doesn't specify somebody's gender.

Gendered	Gender-Neutral
Woman/man/girl/boy	Person
Daughter/son	Child
Mother/father	Parent
Sister/brother	Sibling
Niece/nephew	Nibling

Another identity is called genderfluid.

This is FINN.

Finn shifts between feeling like a girl or a boy.

Some days they feel slightly more like a girl, and other days they feel slightly more like a boy.

Their gender is fluid, which means it can change direction over time, just like the wind or the clouds in the sky!

For Finn, this happens from day to day, but everyone's gender identity can change throughout their life at different moments.

Here are some gender identities and what they mean.

Remember that sometimes people will have their own definitions for these, and that's okay too!

The best thing to do when somebody uses a specific label is to ask them what it means to **them**.

TRANS WOMAN: A WOMAN WHO WAS ASSIGNED MALE AT BIRTH.

TRANS MAN: A MAN WHO WAS ASSIGNED FEMALE AT BIRTH.

NONBINARY: A PERSON WHOSE GENDER ISN'T STRICTLY MALE OR FEMALE BUT SOMETHING ELSE.

AGENDER: A PERSON WHO DOESN'T HAVE ANY PARTICULAR GENDER.

BIGENDER: A PERSON WHO HAS TWO GENDERS. THIS CAN BE BOTH MAN AND WOMAN, MAN AND SOMETHING ELSE, WOMAN AND SOMETHING ELSE, TWO OTHER GENDERS ENTIRELY. YOU GET IT!

GENDERFLUID: A PERSON WHOSE GENDER CHANGES OVER TIME.

GENDERQUEER: A PERSON WHOSE GENDER ISN'T STRICTLY MALE OR FEMALE BUT CAN BE NEITHER, BOTH, OR A COMBINATION.

DEMIGENDER: A PERSON WHO FEELS A SLIGHT CONNECTION TO A GENDER BUT DOESN'T IDENTIFY WITH IT ENTIRELY—FOR EXAMPLE, DEMIGIRL OR DEMIBOY.

GENDERFLUX: A PERSON WHOSE GENDER CHANGES IN INTENSITY OVER TIME, LIKE A LIGHT THAT SHINES VERY BRIGHTLY SOME OF THE TIME AND MORE DIMLY AT OTHERS.

NEUTROIS: A PERSON WHO HAS A NEUTRAL GENDER IDENTITY.

ANDROGYNE: A PERSON WHOSE GENDER IS BOTH MALE AND FEMALE AT THE SAME TIME.

POLYGENDER: A PERSON WHO HAS MULTIPLE GENDER IDENTITIES.

PANGENDER: A PERSON WHO DOESN'T JUST HAVE ONE GENDER BUT CAN IDENTIFY WITH ALL GENDERS AT THE SAME TIME. PAN-MEANS "ALL."

A popular way to describe the word *transgender* is as an umbrella term, meaning it covers lots of different identities that fall under it. These identities can be binary or nonbinary, and it looks a little like this:

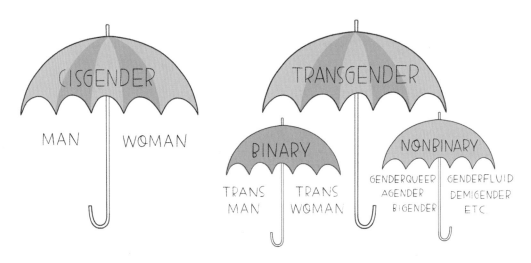

Anyone whose gender identity doesn't exclusively match the sex they were assigned at birth can call themselves transgender.

Some nonbinary people, however, don't like to use the word *transgender*, and they feel like they fit better somewhere outside of cis and trans entirely.

You don't always need to have a specific name for what you're feeling. Some people like having a label. It helps them find other people like them!

Sometimes, though, a label can feel restrictive or uncomfortable. It's okay to not have one!

Sometimes as you grow up, labels and feelings change, and you might feel like you want to switch from one to another or from something to nothing.

All of these are okay! You know yourself best.

The only "right" or "correct" option is where **you** feel the happiest and the most comfortable in your own skin.

NOW WE KNOW

Your gender identity describes who you are on the **inside**, where you feel you belong on the spectrum of girl, boy, transgender, cisgender, or nonbinary.

Transgender and *nonbinary* are umbrella terms that cover lots of different identities.

A nonbinary person can consider themselves transgender but doesn't have to.

Some people like having a label for their gender identity, but if labels make you uncomfortable, you don't have to pick one.

What matters most is that you feel happy.

You know yourself best.

QUESTIONS

♡ What gender do other people call you?

♡ Do you feel like this word fits who you are?

♡ Are there any words from this chapter that feel like they fit how you feel? If not, can you make one up?

♡ Do you know anyone who uses any of the words in this chapter for themselves? Does their meaning for the word match the one in this book, or do they have their own?

CHAPTER 3
THE
GENDER BINARY

In the last chapter, we talked a little about the gender binary, or the idea that girl and boy are the only two genders.

You might be asking yourself, *Who came up with this idea that there are only two sexes and two genders?*

Well...we did. "We" as in people who all live together in a society.

The gender binary is a social construct.

WHAT'S THAT WORD?

A social construct means something was
"constructed" or built by people living in a society.
It doesn't happen in nature on its own, but it's made
up by people based on how they interact. Things like
money, marriage, and borders are social constructs.
Social constructs are given power and meaning
by people living in a society.

But how can believing in the gender binary hurt us?

There are a few reasons, so let's explore these together!

1. The gender binary leaves out people who don't fall neatly into the boxes of girl or boy, people like Max and Finn, for instance.

Think of these examples. Is there ever another option besides "girls" and "boys" to choose from?

★ Sports teams

★ Bathrooms

★ Changing rooms at the gym or pool

★ Gender options on official forms and documents

★ Clothing departments

★ Doctors' offices

Not fitting into one of the options can feel very lonely and uncomfortable.

Sometimes it even means you can't find the things you need, like a doctor or a bathroom to go to.

2. For kids, what activities we're encouraged to do can affect who we might grow up to be.

The more you practice something, the better you get.

If adults only ever encourage you to do things that are considered "appropriate" for your gender, it makes sense that you'll be better at those things.

But you don't really get a chance to try out all the options! For example, Tasha and Trevor both like to play with robot toys.

When Trevor plays with robots, people respond one way.

LOOK AT OUR SMART FUTURE SCIENTIST!

When Tasha joins, people respond a different way.

Trevor is encouraged and keeps playing, while Tasha gets discouraged and moves on to other toys.

3. People who *do* fall into the box of girl or boy might be pushed to do stuff that doesn't really fit them.

Tasha likes to ride her mountain bike and play in nature, but she's been told before that it's not "ladylike" and she should find a quieter hobby.

Adults are also expected to do certain things based on their gender.

Women are often expected to get married and have kids and be more sensitive.

Men are expected to make more money and be tougher.

Over time, expectations like this have led to women being paid less than men for the same jobs and to men being less likely to seek help and therapy if they need it.

THAT DOESN'T SEEM FAIR.

These ideas about what men and women should do are all part of a bigger system called the patriarchy.

WHAT'S THAT WORD?

Patriarchy is the idea that men should have more power and responsibility than anyone else, based on men being the head of a family.

Patriarchy → the rule of the father

Think of US presidents, rich CEOs, and lawmakers. They're mostly men!

I MAKE THE RULES FOR EVERYONE!

4. Western colonization brought about the gender binary as we know it.

Indigenous cultures have always had their own way of defining and categorizing gender. The gender binary as we experience it today started in Europe, and white Europeans spread it to other continents and islands through colonization.

WHAT'S THAT WORD?

Colonization happens when big groups of people from one country settle in another, using that country for resources and spreading their own ideas and beliefs over the ones that were already there.

Because of this, we're at risk of losing older and more expansive gender categories in cultures that may have been more accepting of trans and non-binary people, or having those cultures misrepresented or invalidated.

In this section you will find examples of some identities that exist around the world. It's important to mention these because it shows that if you are trans or nonbinary, you are not alone. There are many people all over the world who feel the same way, and we have a long and rich history of existing everywhere.

Just as gender categories can vary all over the world, people can also experience gender differently based on where they come from and who they are. Things like your religion, your skin color, the country you were born in, or the culture you grew up in can influence what you were taught about gender and how you experience it. This is also called intersectionality.

WHAT'S THAT WORD?

Intersectionality is the idea that all parts of a person's identity influence one another, and that each of us sits at the intersection, or crossroads, of all our different experiences.

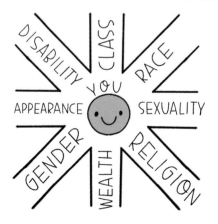

Two-Spirit: a term used for identities in different Indigenous Nations in what is now North and Central America to describe people who fall outside the categories of man or woman. The term was chosen to distinguish these identities from people who are not Indigenous, and it should therefore only be used for Indigenous people.

Māhū: identity in Hawaii and Tahiti, describing people who fall into a third category that is between man and woman or a mix of both. Māhū means "in the middle." Traditionally, māhū were respected teachers and healers.

Fa'afafine: identity in American Samoa, describing people who were assigned male at birth but take on a more feminine role in society. Fa'afafine means "in the manner of a woman" in Samoan.

Fa'afatama: identity in American Samoa, describing people who were assigned female at birth but take on a more masculine role in society. Fa'afatama means "in the manner of a man" in Samoan.

Muxe: identity in Mexico, a word used by the Zapotec people to describe someone who was assigned male at birth but has a more feminine gender expression.

Hijra: identity in South Asian countries, describing someone who was assigned male at birth but has a feminine gender expression. Hijras are legally recognized as their own gender in Nepal, Pakistan, India, and Bangladesh.

The Bugis people of Indonesia recognize five different genders that all need to exist together in harmony.

★ oroané: comparable to cisgender men

★ makkunrai: comparable to cisgender women

★ calalai: comparable to transgender men

★ calabai: comparable to transgender women

★ bissu: people who fall outside of the category of man or woman. also described as combining elements of all genders into one person. They can be intersex. but this is not always the case.

NOW WE KNOW

The idea that our society has two genders and everybody has to be one of those two genders is called the gender binary.

The gender binary divides people into two groups based on the sex assigned at birth. It is a social construct, which means it was made up by people living together in a society and can develop and change over time.

The gender binary can be harmful for the following reasons:

★ It excludes people who fall outside it.

★ It pushes people into gender roles they might not like where they don't fully get to be themselves.

★ It puts gender categories used by cultures around the world at risk of ceasing to exist.

QUESTIONS

♥ What are some situations where a group of people is divided into girls and boys?

♥ Do any of these situations require you to know the sex of the person? If so, why?

♥ Imagine you weren't part of either group but still had to pick one option. What do you think that would feel like?

♥ If we need to divide people into two groups— for example, into teams or for an assignment— what are some other ways this could happen?

CHAPTER 4
GENDER EXPRESSION &
EXPLORATION

Gender identity is who you know you are on the inside.

How you show this on the outside is called gender expression!

There are lots of different ways to do this:

★ Clothing

★ Hair

★ Makeup

★ Interests → what you like

★ Mannerisms → how you act

Tasha, for example, is a cisgender girl. She doesn't love wearing skirts or dresses and feels much more comfortable in pants.

This is Tasha in her favorite pair of overalls! She can run, jump, climb, and bike in them, and they haven't torn once!

She likes being in nature, playing with her dog, and drawing all the different flowers she sees.

Tasha likes to wear her hair long and natural, and her favorite hairdo is pigtail puffs.

These are all part of Tasha's gender expression.

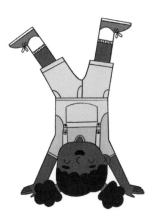

Veronica is a trans girl. She likes to wear her hair short and really enjoys wearing skirts and dresses.

She especially likes colorful prints. They make her feel fancy and festive, and the patterns are bright and cheerful, like her personality!

Veronica likes video games and dancing, and her favorite subject is English.

Max is nonbinary. They like big comfy sweaters that stretch over their hands.

They really like frogs and mushrooms, and they love giving the wheels of their wheelchair colorful spokes.

They also love science and learning about space.

Finn is genderfluid, meaning their feelings about their gender change.

Some days, Finn likes wearing dresses and skirts. Other days, they prefer pants and a T-shirt.

Finn likes baseball, playing guitar, and their cat, Georgie. Sometimes they wear a pin to tell other people what they would like to be called that day.

This is Billy. Billy is a cisgender boy.

He likes wearing dresses and skirts because they make him happy!

He really likes making up his own stories and hopes that one day he can write a book!

Billy and Tasha are examples of people whose gender expressions are different from what is expected of their gender identity. This is also called being gender nonconforming.

WHAT'S THAT WORD?

Being gender nonconforming means you don't stick to (that is, you don't conform to) the rules people have made up about gender, in this case that girls have to wear skirts and boys have to wear pants.

Unfortunately, it's often seen as less okay for boys to like "girl" things than the other way around. Which brings us to something very important...

I'm going to let you in on a secret.

No matter what other people say...there are actually no "boy" or "girl" things! Since the gender binary is a social construct with made-up rules, everything can be for everybody!

GIRL CLOTHES & BOY CLOTHES, JUST CLOTHES

GIRL
TOYS
& BOY
TOYS
JUST ↳
TOYS

GIRL
HOBBIES
& BOY
HOBBIES,
JUST ↳
HOBBIES

Like we saw with Billy, somebody's gender expression doesn't always match their gender identity.

Looks don't always show who a person is on the inside; they're just the tip of the iceberg of who a person really is.

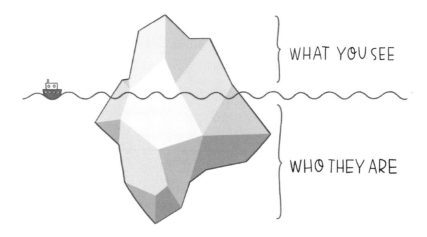

WHAT YOU SEE

WHO THEY ARE

When you see someone in public or meet someone new, try not to assume who they are just from what they look like!

There are lots of reasons why somebody might not be dressing exactly as they want to. They might not feel safe or ready yet, or might not have access to the things they need to change their appearance.

Other people might not want to change their appearance at all and are perfectly happy continuing to present the same way.

Some trans and nonbinary people may feel uncomfortable in the body they were born with or with the way this makes other people see them.

This is called gender dysphoria.

WHAT'S THAT WORD?

Gender dysphoria describes the anxiety somebody feels when the sex they were assigned at birth and the gender they know themselves to be don't match.

Dysphoros→ difficult to bear

Gender dysphoria can be two things:

★ Physical: related to your body and its parts

★ Social: related to what people call you, how they talk about you, and how they see you

To help with gender dysphoria, some people choose to transition.

WHAT'S THAT WORD?

> Transitioning is the process of changing from one way of being to another. In the case of a trans person, this means taking steps to change things about your body or your life in general that will help you be your true gender identity.

Just like gender dysphoria, transitioning can be physical and/or social.

There are many ways to transition, for example:

NEW NAME + PRONOUNS

NEW HAIRCUT

HELLO, MY NAME IS:

NEW CLOTHES + ACCESSORIES

Physical transitioning is sometimes also called medical transitioning, as it can involve doctors and nurses. Trans people might want to take hormones or undergo specific surgeries to make their bodies match how they feel.

Some people choose to go this way, but not everyone does, and it's important to remember that changing things about one's appearance doesn't make a person any more or less trans or valid.

It's always important to do what makes you the most comfortable and happy.

Social transitioning is about what words you use for yourself, how you'd like other people to see you, and what you'd like other people to call you—for example, going by a different name or pronouns.

Pronouns are the words people use to refer to you when they're not using your name.

Here are some examples of different pronouns people use!

HE	HIM	HIS	HIS	HIMSELF
SHE	HER	HER	HERS	HERSELF
THEY	THEM	THEIR	THEIRS	THEMSELF
ZE	ZIR	ZIR	ZIRS	ZIRSELF
SIE	HIR	HIR	HIRS	HIRSELF
XE	XEM	XYR	XYRS	XEMSELF
E/EY	EM	EIR	EIRS	EIRSELF
IT	IT	ITS	ITS	ITSELF
AE	AER	AER	AERS	AERSELF
FAE	FAER	FAER	FAERS	FAERSELF

If somebody uses multiple sets of pronouns, usually it means you can use them alongside one another! To make extra sure, it's always okay to ask what someone prefers.

On the other side of feelings about gender is gender euphoria!

WHAT'S THAT WORD?

Gender euphoria is the feeling of being intensely happy or excited about your gender.

Euphoros → happy or healthy

Gender euphoria happens when your gender expression feels perfectly aligned with your gender identity—for example, your appearance or pronouns—and it makes you feel happy, comfortable, and relieved.

They/them pronouns

Sometimes people don't want to use *they/them* pronouns for a single person because they think it doesn't make sense in English grammar (even though it actually does).

Think about these sentences. We use *they/them* for one person all the time!

Singular *they* first appeared in written form in 1375, which probably means it was used in spoken language even earlier.

When somebody uses the wrong pronouns for somebody, this is called misgendering.

WHAT'S THAT WORD?

To misgender somebody means to refer to them with a word or a name that doesn't reflect their true identity. Misgendering can feel really icky because it shows that the picture others have of someone might not match who they really are.

If you accidentally misgender somebody, just say thank you when they correct you and change your language! It can happen to anyone, and moving on quickly is usually the best thing to do.

If somebody misgenders you, it's okay to correct them! If you can't, take care of yourself and do something that will make you feel better.

If you're not sure what pronouns to use for somebody, it's usually okay to ask in a nice and polite way, or try introducing yourself with your own pronouns first!

Something to Remember

Somebody else's view of you does not change who you are and what you know about yourself.

It's also important to use neutral language whenever you can. It's a good way to make sure nobody feels left out and that you don't accidentally misgender somebody.

Try some of the options below when talking to a group of people!

INSTEAD OF:

LADIES AND GENTLEMEN.

BOYS AND GIRLS.

TRY:

HEY, FRIENDS!

HELLO, EVERYONE!

HI, Y'ALL!

DEAR GUESTS/ STUDENTS/ PASSENGERS.

GREETINGS, FELLOW HUMANS.

Self-discovery

You might be wondering at this point, *How do I know whether I'm cis, trans, nonbinary, or something else?*

You're the only one who can answer that question. It's something you'll learn about yourself over time, or maybe you already have some idea.

You'll probably read more books after this one and talk to quite a few people, but eventually you'll be able to come up with an answer.

And it's okay if that answer changes.

A good way to learn about yourself is to try things out! Experiment with different looks and likes, and see what makes you feel best about yourself.

★ Create a video game character that feels like you.

★ Draw yourself in a way that feels most like you.

★ Go through a workbook and answer questions.

★ Try dressing up in different clothes.

You can do this by yourself, with a friend, or with an adult you trust.

NOW WE KNOW

Gender expression is how we choose to show the world our gender identity, who we are on the inside.

This can fit with ideas we have about gender roles, but it doesn't have to!

Not everyone is able to dress the way they would like to, so it's important not to make assumptions based on somebody's looks.

Being trans or nonbinary also doesn't have a set appearance. The most important thing is to be comfortable and happy!

Some trans and nonbinary people choose to make more permanent changes to their bodies to feel more comfortable, but not everybody does.

When approaching new people or speaking to a group, it's polite to ask for their pronouns or speak with more neutral words, so everyone can feel included.

QUESTIONS

♥ What gender do you see yourself as?

♥ How do you think other people see you?

♥ Do you think there are differences between the two?

♥ What would you like others to see when they look at you?

♥ What kind of clothing or hairstyle do you feel comfortable wearing? What style makes you happy?

♥ Think about people around you. Who do you feel similar to? Who do you look up to and see yourself growing up as?

♥ With whom or where do you feel safest expressing yourself?

CHAPTER 5
CHALLENGES &
SUPPORT

In a world where so much is influenced by the gender binary, challenging it can cause you to have to jump some extra hurdles along the way.

This chapter will go over some of the challenges you might encounter and how you can find the support you need to get through them.

COMING OUT

A really common challenge you hear about when it comes to gender and sexuality is coming out.

WHAT'S THAT WORD?

Coming out means you're telling somebody your gender identity or sexuality if you are not cisgender and/or straight.

MOM, I THINK I MIGHT BE NONBINARY.

It's often quite scary as you don't know how another person will react or what they will say.

Some things about coming out:

★ Think about who you'd like to tell. Who do you trust? Who do you think will understand?

★ You don't have to tell anyone anything you don't want to, and you don't need to come out to anyone if you're not ready or don't feel safe.

★ It's also okay if you're not completely sure. Talking to other people could help you understand yourself better.

★ Think of questions the person might ask, and have some answers ready. You can also give them resources (like this book!) that might help them understand.

★ You'll probably come out more than once, in lots of new situations and with lots of new people you meet.

★ If a question makes you uncomfortable or you don't know the answer, it's okay to say that!

★ It's not your job to educate everyone. Some people might feel entitled to information from you, especially if you're the only trans or nonbinary person they know. It's not your responsibility to have all the answers ready for them, and it's okay to tell them you can't speak for everyone and that they can find their answers from other resources.

★ Coming out can be scary, but it can also lead to very good things if it means you can get the support you need!

No matter how understanding a person is, they will most likely need time to process the information you just told them.

Sometimes grown-ups get sad, uncomfortable, or anxious when they're told something they don't understand.

THANK YOU FOR TELLING ME.

I MIGHT NEED SOME TIME TO ADJUST, BUT I'M HERE FOR YOU.

It's not your fault if they feel this way, and you still deserve to be treated with respect.

I'M ACTUALLY A GIRL.

I CAN'T ACCEPT THIS.

If you're able to, ask friends or an adult if they can support you before and after you talk to people.

PARENTS / GUARDIANS

THERAPIST

TEACHER

DOCTOR

A good way to recognize a grown-up who could help is to look for clues.

Do they talk about the kinds of things we brought up in this book?

ALLY

SAFE SPACE

Do they have stickers or other clues around their office with rainbows or gender symbols?

Do they call out people who are mean to others and offer to help?

Below are some other examples of people who can support you!

SCHOOL COUNSELOR

FRIENDS

SIBLINGS

If somebody comes out to *you*, here are some good things to remember:

★ This is a big deal! They trusted you enough to share this with you, so make sure you tell them how much you appreciate this.

★ Listen to them: Their feelings are important!

★ Believe them: They know themselves best, just like you know yourself best.

★ Ask questions: Different words mean different things to different people, and it's always better to ask than to assume.

★ You can say, "What does that word mean to you?"

★ Be respectful: Call a person what they would like to be called. Don't ask questions about their body: they still deserve privacy!

★ A good rule to follow: If you wouldn't want a stranger to ask **you** something, maybe don't ask someone else either.

★ Do some research: It's not the other person's responsibility to teach you everything, but remember to check in and see if what you find is true for them.

GATEKEEPING

Gatekeeping is the act of limiting access to something.

Imagine somebody holding a gate closed and stopping you from going through.

When grown-ups think kids are too young to learn or know about gender identity, this is called gatekeeping.

Gender is all around us and influences so many things we do and learn. Talking about it early means we can find out what parts we like and what parts we don't.

Learning about gender also helps you find the right words to talk about who you are and what you're feeling, and helps you better understand other people.

Sometimes doctors, people who make laws, or other people in power are the ones who gatekeep.

For example, they might try to prevent you from seeking medical help, using the bathroom you want, or accessing information because they don't respect your identity.

This is also called transphobia.

WHAT'S THAT WORD?

Transphobia is an irrational fear or dislike of trans people. People who are transphobic believe there is something wrong with trans people and that they don't deserve basic rights.

Transphobia → trans = short for *transgender*, phobia = fear

If this sounds crummy and hopeless, believe me, I understand. Things can be tough, but know there are countless adults (like me!) out there who *do* believe you and are fighting for your rights.

SCHOOL & BULLYING

School and other public places can have some hurdles to jump as well.

Lots of places have bathrooms or locker rooms that are divided into girls' and boys', or activities split up by assumed gender.

EVERYONE DIVIDE INTO BOYS AND GIRLS!

It can feel really uncomfortable to be forced into a space where you don't feel you fit and that doesn't match who you are.

If you're able to and feel safe, you can suggest ways that could make it better!

It's good to have supportive grown-ups and friends join you as well. More voices speaking together are much louder than just one!

★ Suggest a gender-neutral bathroom.

★ Suggest other ways of dividing people into groups or teams.

★ Remind people that there really is no difference between "girl" and "boy" things: They're just things!

What are some other changes you think could be made?

How would you change them?

Sometimes when people are different from others they can face bullying. Bullying and hurting other people with words or violence is *never* okay.

See if your school has an anti-bullying policy and whether it includes gender identity.

If this happens to you, tell an adult you trust, like a teacher, parent, or guardian. They can also help you research and find resources if you're going through a tough time (you can find some of these in the Resources section at the end of this book).

NAME & PRONOUNS

If you use a different name and pronouns than what you were given when you were born, they might not match everywhere you go.

This can happen at school, at the doctor, or anywhere they need to keep a written record of you.

Again, you can have a helpful adult talk or send an e-mail to the places you'll be visiting and remind them to use the right name and pronouns for you.

MENTAL HEALTH

Because of all the added hurdles, lots of young people struggle with their mental health. It's important to take care of your brain just as much as your body!

Here are some good, positive skills you can use when you're feeling down. Different things work for different people, so find what helps you the most!

★ Keep a journal to write down your thoughts and feelings.

★ Keep a list of what makes you happy and helps you feel better when you're sad. Sometimes it's hard to remember these things when we're not okay.

★ Try finding a distraction or doing something that will make you laugh, like watching cute animal videos, playing a game, or reading a book.

★ If there's somebody you can talk to, ask them if it's okay to confide in them.

★ Reach out to a professional! You can't and shouldn't have to handle everything alone.

★ Support groups, therapy, and counseling are amazing resources. You can talk to somebody who specializes in the things you're going through, and they can help you overcome challenges, process your feelings, and talk to others.

I hope that this book has been able to explain lots of stuff about gender identity, and has helped you understand yourself and others a little bit better.

I'm going to leave you with just a few thoughts.

YOU ARE RIGHT JUST AS YOU ARE.

YOU DESERVE TO BE RESPECTED AND TO FEEL HAPPY, SAFE, AND COMFORTABLE.

YOUR IDENTITY AND HOW YOU FEEL ABOUT YOURSELF ARE VALID.

EVERYONE DESERVES TO BE ACCEPTED FOR WHO THEY ARE.

GO OUT THERE AND KEEP BEING AMAZING!

Author's Note

My goal for this book was to provide a friendly, accessible, and inclusive introduction to the concept of gender identity to you, the reader. Maybe you're questioning or wanting to explore your own identity, maybe a friend or family member came out to you and you want to know how to support them, or maybe you saw something on the news about transgender and nonbinary people and aren't quite sure what that means. My hope is that this book will feel like an open conversation with a friend, providing information without judgment and with plenty of room for questions, exploration, and further research should you need it. I also wrote this book with the understanding that terms and definitions may change over time, and feedback and conversations to improve inclusiveness are always welcomed.

Sources and additional reading are listed in the back of the book, but there are a few extra credits that are better explained in an author's note. The trans umbrella drawing on page 38 has been used far and wide by many people and organizations, so I decided to adapt it for this book as well, as it's a great visual explanation. The analogy I use in this book to explain the spectrum and fluidity of gender are colors and mixing paint, but you should also check out the *Robot Hugs* webcomic called "Gender Scoop," which explains those in ice-cream flavors! Finally, the concept of intersectionality explained on page 51 was first pioneered by Black feminist scholar Kimberlé Crenshaw in 1989.

Who am I?

My name is Andy, and I'm a nonbinary person in my early thirties. Nonbinary to me means that I don't fully belong into the category of either man or woman, but somewhere in between. I use *they/them* pronouns, so for example you could say, "This is Andy, and they wrote this book!" I was born in the Netherlands and grew up in different countries all over the world before settling in the US in my early twenties. This is where I first met other people who were transgender and non-binary, and something clicked. We had so much in common, and I'd always felt something was off in the way I was expected to present to the world in terms of my assigned gender. Learning that the word *nonbinary* existed and could apply to me was like opening a window in a stuffy room and finally being able to breathe. Whatever this book and the words explained in it end up meaning to you, I'm happy and grateful that you decided to pick it up.

Acknowledgments

I want to thank Little, Brown Books for Young Readers for tackling this project with me and giving me the opportunity to publish it, specifically Andrea Colvin, Regan Winter, Aria Balraj, and Lauren Kisare. Thank you to my agent, Alex Gehringer, for presenting this concept to lots and lots of people before we were able to make it happen, and to Buzz Slutsky for providing an amazing sensitivity read. Finally, thank you to the generations of transgender, nonbinary, and gender expansive people that came before me—I thought about you a lot while writing this, and I hope this book helps to foster a world that is increasingly more welcoming and understanding.

Resources

Picture Books

Being You: A First Conversation About Gender, written by Megan Madison and Jessica Ralli, illustrated by Andy Passchier (Rise x Penguin Workshop, 2022)

The Gender Wheel, by Maya Gonzalez (Reflection Press, 2018)

It Feels Good to Be Yourself, written by Theresa Thorn, illustrated by Noah Grigni (Henry Holt and Company, 2019)

A Kids Book About Gender, by Dale Mueller (A Kids Company About Inc., 2020)

Pink Is for Boys, written by Robb Pearlman, illustrated by Eda Kaban (Running Press Kids, 2018)

What Are Your Words? A Book About Pronouns, written by Katherine Locke, illustrated by Anne Passchier (Little, Brown Books for Young Readers, 2021)

Who Are You? A Kid's Guide to Gender Identity, written by Brook Pessin-Whedbee, illustrated by Naomi Bardoff (Jessica Kingsley Publishers, 2016)

Teens and Adults

Beyond the Gender Binary, by Alok Vaid-Menon (Penguin Workshop, 2020)

How to Understand Your Gender: A Practical Guide for Exploring Who You Are written by Alex Iantaffi and Meg-John Barker (Jessica Kingsley Publishers, 2018)

A Quick & Easy Guide to They/Them Pronouns, by Archie Bongiovanni and Tristan Jimerson (Limerence Press, 2018)

A Quick & Easy Guide to Queer & Trans Identities, by Mady G. and J.R. Zuckerberg (Limerence Press, 2019)

Trans+: Love, Sex, Romance, and Being You, by Kathryn Gonzales and Karen Rayne (Magination Press, 2019)

They/Them/Their: A Guide to Nonbinary & Genderqueer Identities, by Eris Young (Jessica Kingsley Publishers, 2020)

Trans Bodies, Trans Selves: A Resource for the Transgender Community, edited by Laura Erickson-Schroth (Oxford University Press, 2014)

For People Supporting Gender Creative Kids

The Gender Creative Child: Pathways for Nurturing and Supporting Children Who Live Outside Gender Boxes, by Diane Ehrensaft (The Experiment, 2016)

Raising My Rainbow: Adventures in Raising a Fabulous, Gender Creative Son, Lori Duron (Broadway Books, 2013)

Raising the Transgender Child: A Complete Guide for Parents, Families & Caregivers, by Michelle Angelo and Ali Bowman (Seal Press, 2016)

Raising Them: Our Adventure in Gender Creative Parenting, by Kyl Myers (TOPPLE BOOKS & Little A, 2020)

Workbooks

The Gender Identity Workbook for Kids: A Guide to Exploring Who You Are, written by Kelly Storck, illustrated by Noah Grigni (Instant Help, 2018)

The Gender Quest Workbook: A Guide for Teens and Young Adults Exploring Gender Identity, by Rylan Jay Testa, Deborah Coolhart, and Jayme Peta (Instant Help, 2015)

Web Resources and Organizations

GLSEN.org
genderinfinity.org
genderspectrum.org
HRC.org/resources/schools-in-transition
   -a-guide-for-supporting-transgender
   -students-in-k-12-s
welcomingschools.org
interactadvocates.org
interconnect.support
mermaidsuk.org.uk
transequality.org
transfamilies.org
transhealthproject.org
transyouthequality.org
transstudent.org